Barn Owl

ENCOUNTERS IN THE WILD

JIM CRUMLEY

Saraband

ONE

I WAS VERY YOUNG when I understood why a heart shape symbolises love. It was the shape of the fair face of barn owls – and I loved barn owls.

Prefab childhood in 1950s Dundee was essentially lived more out of doors than in. The prefabs were neatly buttoned to a west-facing hillside along the last street in town, and the farmland of Angus began across the road. Fields were as much for playing in as growing crops. From the top of the highest fields the land fell away northwards and rose again to the promise of the Sidlaw Hills. I considered winter geese and spring and summer skylarks to be as much my neighbours as my fellow prefab-dwellers ever were.

The entrance to the farmyard was no more than a quarter of a mile away from our prefab, but it was forbidden territory, and inhabited by what Lewis Grassic Gibbon would have called "coarse brutes". Thinking about it now, they must have been simply people who did not know how to get on with the non-farming neighbours surrounding them on three sides. I hid when I saw them coming, though it does me no good to admit it now. One of them, only slightly older than myself, once opened a nasty cut in the side of my leg with an astonishingly well-aimed stone.

But the stackyard was a different proposition from the farmyard. I thought of it as no-man's land. It belonged to the farm, of course, and farming things happened there, but it was frontier land that lay between the farmyard and the street from which it was only flimsily fenced off. And mine was the kind of childhood that did not pay much heed to flimsy fences.

Haystacks were shifting, unchancy creatures, especially at night. They seemed to appear overnight then stood around for weeks, or months, and grew dishevelled in gales and downpours. Voles, mice and rats and other furry beasts I couldn't name sped along the curved alleyways between stacks, and barn owls loved voles, mice and rats as much as I loved barn owls, albeit a different kind of love.

So my first barn owls coursed silently through my most impressionable years, low-flying, head-down hunters that tilted and swerved on one wingtip or the other as the light faded over the Tay estuary far below and the lights of villages on its Fife shore glittered in small clusters. The darker the night, the brighter the face, the breast and the underwings of the moping, mopping-up owl, and the more predatory its grip on my young imagination.

◉ ◉ ◉

THE FARM (it seems to me now) was a poor, run-down place with run-down barns, and these are the barn owl's favourite kind. Any evening I happened to be walking home that way (and always just a little heart-in-mouth at the proximity of the forbidden territory), there was always the chance of meeting head-on and at close quarters the fair, heart-shaped face of the haunter of no-man's land. These were encounters with nature at the edge of things, the edge of the day and night and the edge of my comfort zone, beyond which the black outline of the farm buildings bleakly inked in my discomfort zone.

◉ ◉ ◉

THE EDGE OF THINGS has since become my preferred terrain – the edge of the land, the edge of the sea, islands beyond the edge of the land, the Highland edge and the Lowland edge wherever the two have been in constant collision for… well, since the world began, but the last ten thousand years will do for the moment and the sake of argument; wherever the tribes of nature rub shoulders and overlap – wherever Highland eyes Lowland and a golden eagle arrows down a fast mile from the first and last mountain to lift a dainty pink-footed goose from the first and last tilting field, the goose deceived into thinking it was just a buzzard until it was much too late; wherever a shoreline-hunting fox might stare out at the ocean with ears forward to catch the cadences of a singing humpback whale.

The barn owl is an ambassador for life on the edge. It is the night owl that also hunts fearlessly by day; the silent flier with a sudden shriek that can shatter glass (and in the brain of a short-tailed field vole it must sound like the shrill anthem of death itself); the restless sentry of the outside edge of the woods with one ear attuned to the grassy banks and the other to the first and last tree shadows; the stone-still embellishment on a country kirkyard gravestone beyond the edge of the village, looking in moonlight like nothing so much as the sculptor's final inspired flourish.

☉ ☉ ☉

ENCOUNTERS IN THE WILD

ALL THIS I CAN SEE CLEARLY NOW as a line drawn across the map of my life, a line that began in the stackyard of childhood, although of course the line truly began long before it first crossed my wandering, wondering path, began back on the dwindling edge of the last ice, the edge of the first woods after the ice, the edge of the first settlements along the edge of the first woods, the edge of the first group of stone buildings, the edge of the first farms, stackyards, estate buildings, clock towers that rose purposefully and ticked away the seasons of the centuries until they fell into disuse. It quested among all the new edges of the advance of the people, until, in the late-twentieth and the early-twenty-first centuries the people realised that they could counter the worst side-effects of intensive agriculture, not to mention farmyard renovations and conversions from barns into houses, by building barn owl nest boxes in new metal-roofed barns and in the trees near the edges of new woods and old.

Thus, in the course of one nature writer's life, the barn owl's capacity for exploiting the edge of things (however and wherever the edge evolves) has allowed it to recover from every setback and to thrive again where less accommodating creatures have succumbed. And because I am a traveller along the edge of things myself, I have been accustomed for much of my life to meeting barn owls along the way.

Those childhood barn owls survive only as a patchwork of memories, memories of glimpses, as unrevealing as moths darting in from the darkness to dance at a flame and vanish again. I remember nothing other than impressions of a few seconds of flight at a time, usually into the insipid glow of street lights, then fading away into the gloom, always fading away into that other world where owl and farmyard conspired to do whatever it was they did together. Except once.

That once was when I was lured by forces beyond my control across no-man's land and into hostile territory, the forbidden world beyond the haystacks. It was the first time I ever saw the owl fly in daylight. It was a sunny early morning of spring although why I might have been near the farm in early morning escapes me now. The owl had appeared among the stacks with its beak clamped round a mouse that hung down from its heart-shaped face like a moustache (a mouse-tache), and I had not seen *that* before either. It flew away round the corner of the nearest building, vanished, then reappeared a few seconds later, spotlit by the sun against the dark background of a second building on the far side of the farmyard. I had never so much as looked at that building before, but now I saw that its door leaned open at an odd angle and that through the doorway I could see gaps in the slate roof. The owl banked left and flew inside. This was new intelligence. An owl that lived *inside* a building was not a possibility that had ever occurred to me before.

Moments later it was out again, and clean-shaven (the mouse-tache had gone). Even at that tender age I understood nests and had found skylark, blackbird, chaffinch and robin nests within half a mile of home, sparrow nests in the garden hedge. And I knew that kittiwakes (already one of my favourite words) nested on sea cliffs out by Arbroath. I understood something of how they worked, but they were all *outside*, in the grass, the bushes, the hedges, or staring out to sea. I was still coming to terms with the problem of a bird that lived in a building when a second barn owl flew out from the broken-down door of the broken-down barn.

My first thought was that it might be a brother, because I had one, and we were accustomed to going in and out of a building by the same door. Then an owl flew back in. The same owl? The first owl? Another owl altogether? How many owls were in there and why was the building so important to them? Before I knew what was happening (and years before I *understood* what was happening), I was in among the haystacks and heading for the corner of the nearest farm building. I flattened against the wall (I had seen people do this in films) and peered tentatively round the corner. Coast clear (I had heard people say this in films). I inched sideways along the gable end to the next corner where it suddenly became clear that I was deep in forbidden territory, and that between me and the owl door of the owl building was a wide open space deeply rutted with mud and liberally dowsed with cowshit, which at the time I would have politely called "country pancakes". Almost certainly, I would have been wearing Clark's sandals, short socks and short trousers. I was not dressed for this.

If there had been people moving around, if there had been tractors, horses, herds of cows, or any one of the awful tribe of coarse, stone-throwing brutes, I would have lost my nerve and run. But there was no-one and nothing moving. The smell was what troubled me most at that moment, but a bad smell was no worse than a flimsy fence. I ran across the farmyard and straight in the door of the barn. It was almost underworld-black in there after the sunlit overworld where glowing birds with white, heart-shaped faces flew. At first, all was shadow, gloom, chaos, I bumped into things, then something muttered from somewhere up near the roof. I looked up into a white, heart-shaped face, and in that moment, the barn owl claimed me as a friend for life.

It tilted its head at right angles, so that the heart-shaped face looked like a butterfly, then straightened up again. It was, I decided, a conjuring trick. It was, unquestionably, magic.

The owl was standing on a kind of wooden shelf where the wall met the roof. Right next to where it stood was a curious low pile of grey stuff that looked like a cross between wool and used Brillo pads. It would take years before I realised what it was and what it was made of.

Then a second owl drifted past me somewhere near the floor and rose without a sound to the same shelf and stood beside the first owl, then both birds did the sideways head trick again, and I wanted to clap. Then the second owl sat on the pile of grey stuff. Then a tractor engine fired up in the distance and my awareness of where I was and what I was doing and what would happen to me if I was caught rushed in the door like an icy wind. The owl-spell was shattered and I had wings on my feet. I was over the fence and most of the way home before I stopped running.

"I fell in the field," I explained to my mother as she first looked at me then caught the scent of cows. But something fundamental took root that day and I reap its consequences still. I had charged into no-man's land, crossed enemy lines, lived to tell the tale and returned a warrior for nature's cause. Barn owls did that.

◉ ◉ ◉

THE PREFABS, the farmyard, the stackyard and all the fields have long since been obliterated by housing and a major hospital. The barn owls retreated beyond the redefined boundaries of suburbia.

TWO

THE COTTAGE IS A RUIN on the steep side of a quiet, south-facing fold in the Ochil Hills immediately to the north-east of Stirling. I met an old shepherd there once who told me it was lived in as recently as the 1950s. If that is true, its dereliction has been swift and is now almost complete. The roof is gone without trace. The front wall is all but gone, two broken stone doorposts and a windowsill (but not the window) give some sense of what it might have looked like. The back wall is only slightly less decrepit. The gables still stand, but every winter they crumble a little more. The cottage would have had one-and-a-half storeys, a sleeping platform in the roof.

It is utterly alone at the end of a mile-long meandering track that connects to a single-track road across the west edge of the Ochils. There is no other house at all anywhere within these hills. For company it has only the rowan tree a few yards from the front door which was planted purposefully there, for such is the tradition hereabouts: a rowan by the house wards off unwanted spirits and protects all who are welcome here. Part of the track has been re-made now to take hill-farm vehicles and to service the felling of a small plantation of conifers. But the last few hundred yards are still green and narrow and hairpinned. The track fords one hill burn and bridges another, the conduit of another time and symbolically redolent of the lives that were lived here.

I have known the place for forty years. I have walked the track uncounted times, and at least in the early years, I idly fantasised a life for myself in its re-built, re-roofed embrace with a tall column of smoke standing above it on still, frosted nights under a huge moon. In the security of that house in that fold in the hills I would become a child of nature again and write my books. But it occurs to me now that in order to realise that fantasy I would have had to evict the barn owls. Also, I would have had sheep for neighbours, and that wouldn't have worked.

There were two chimneys. The one on the east gable is still in place, or at least enough of it remains to get the gist of it. Chimneys in such places (and especially once the rain and the frost and the wind have started to burst them apart) are perfect nest sites for birds that don't like to build nests. This one was the home of barn owls for at least twenty years that I know of. Then for reasons that I don't know of they disappeared and the neighbourhood kestrels moved from an old crow's nest in the gully trees to the vacant chimney. Now I think the chimney may be too far gone to accommodate anything at all, but I will be happy to be proved wrong.

☉　☉　☉

IN THOSE TWENTY YEARS I never found a more ideal man-made nest site for a barn owl in all my wanderings through my native land, and that remained the case until I came across its kindred spirit three years ago at the end of a long track far out on a quiet headland in the south of the Isle of Skye; kindred spirits united by isolation, by the inexorable ruination of the buildings (the Skye cottage still has some way to go, its roof is still in place but loosening), and by their colonising barn owls once human life had vanished and faded to the very outer edges of living memory.

Geographically, their situations could hardly be more dissimilar. The Ochils cottage, which is mysteriously called Jerah, is tucked into its hillside, sheltered from prevailing winds by the trees that throng the gully of a hoarse hill burn immediately to the west, hemmed in by steep, swooping, rounded hills on three sides, and as determinedly land-locked as any Scottish hillside can be. The Skye cottage, single-storey and low-slung, hunkers down on a bare clifftop wide open to ocean winds from the south-west, and the view from its back "garden" (a piece of land indistinguishable from the surrounding sheep-and-cattle-shorn terrain) stares at the Cuillin, at the mountainous, ocean-going profile of Rum, at sunsets such as you never dared to dream, and all of that was seared into the hearts and minds of hundreds of nineteenth century islanders whose fate was determined by the architects of the Highland Clearances. The barn owls quest restlessly among the waist-high ruins of the abandoned township of Suisnish, whose very name is shorthand for one of the Clearances' blackest episodes. Seabirds scream in the airspace and golden eagles cruise low over the empty miles of the headland. The sea eagles have returned although the people never did, not here.

The cottage, the one with the roof, is later than the cleared ruins. Here too, in another echo of the Ochils cottage, barn owls moved in, and I met an old woman who lived in Torrin back on the road where the track sets out south along the shore of Loch Slapin to Suisnish and the sea. Her father was a postman, and she remembered him delivering mail to the cottage, the cottage which is now the address of barn owls. And I had known that place myself for about twenty-five years before the day I looked in at one windowless window frame and (inducing a shudder of recognition that reverberated all the way back to my Dundee childhood) a barn owl flew out of the nearby doorless doorway.

Both Suisnish and Jerah inhabit landscapes whose natural ecosystems have been largely obliterated by overgrazing. The still-belligerent free-range presence of sheep and cattle torments the ruins and defaces their melancholy inheritance. But that melancholy has surely been mitigated, dignified, beautified by the owls. It is a characteristic of what I think of as the forgiveness of nature. Ours is the only species so hell-bent on taking nature on, hell-bent on taming it, compromising it, obliterating it where it suits us. Yet whenever we turn our backs on some failed human endeavour of despoliation, from Gruinard Island to Chernobyl, nature begins to move in again almost at once, lays ground cover, plants trees, soothes broken stones with moss, summons swallows, dragonflies, orchids, wolves, barn owls.

BARN OWL

Sometimes, in our more lucid moments, we take our cue from nature. Elsewhere on South Skye, in the Ochils, and dozens of other landscapes, native woodland is being restored, and with the trees come new growth, insects, flowers, birds, mammals. Among the countless beneficiaries of such lucidity, barn owls hunt the redefined woodland edge and the open land beyond and the rising or the setting sun turns their white plumage pale pink or pale gold, and something new begins on the land and in the air, or rather, something very old has been restored.

⊙　⊙　⊙

SUISNISH OFFERS rarefied barn owl watching. To be there at sunset and linger on into the gloaming (and if you have the tolerances for it, on into moon-or-star-light) is a rarefied event in itself, for sunset drapes itself over and around the Cuillin ranges of both Rum and Skye, infuses all the intervening tracts and inlets of the Atlantic Ocean, and ignites the very mountains so that they smoulder with echoes of their volcanic infancy. Add to these the passing and lingering tribes of seabirds, from gannets and greater black-backs to fulmars, auks and arctic terns and all their raised voices, overlay these with the soulful chants of eiders and grey seals and you have a box seat in a theatre of enchantment. Was that the wind in a rickle of stones or did you just gasp out loud?

As a stage set it is all so outrageously overdone that it overwhelms watching eyes for want of a focal point. But while my back was turned on the cottage, the hunting barn owl slipped out through the black and vacant doorway, flew round two sides of the cottage (the shadowed front, the ocean-lit south gable end), and burst with devastating slowness and silence into that tingling airspace like a sudden waft of bog-myrtle scent in a new rainfall. And now I had my focal point.

And now with binoculars raised I fed hungrily, a predator gorging on beauty, for the barn owl (which is unarguably beautiful in any light and in no light at all) wore electric copper on its back and upper wings, the back of its neck and upper head, deep pink on its heart-face, breast and underwings; and as it flew south-to-north and crossed the fieriest flare of the afterglow between me and the point where the sun finally ducked down behind Garsbheinn, the whole bird was a shadow rimmed in the most vivid shade of burning gold I have ever seen in forty years of staring out Skye sunsets, forty years in which I finally thought I had reason to believe that neither Skye sunsets nor barn owls for that matter had anything new to show me.

The owl flew on north and out of reach of fiery skies. The moment softly dissolved and the owl began to look like itself again. Yet even then, as I followed it in the glasses, pinnacle after pinnacle of the Skye Cuillin drifted through the background in a blurred but distinctly recognisable pageant of mountainous superstars. At last, the background ran out of mountains, and as if the owl had sensed the lessening of its impact on watcher eyes it wheeled south again, dipped towards the clifftop, and began sifting among the waist-high ruins of the cleared township, unsettling human ghosts and living mice and voles. Occasionally it stopped on the air, lowered long blond legs and feigned a stoop, or thudded softly into the grass or the nettles that thrive within forgetful, broken walls.

The owl's strike rate is not high. In twenty unbroken minutes during which the owl was hardly out of my sight (and never for more than a few seconds at a time), it stooped six times and made no kills. Then it dropped below the level of the clifftop and vanished from my sight and I was left wondering how close to the waves it might descend from time to time and whether it did so at ease or in discomfort, and then I was wondering how conscious it might have been about the rarefied nature of the landscape where it had so recently carved out a territory, and what had persuaded it to come here in the first place and where it had come from, for Hebridean islands and the West Highland mainland, are hardly renowned as barn owl strongholds.

The moment of the owl's descent towards the waves recalled a kestrel I once watched in

Orkney. I saw it several times over a week and it hunted constantly along the very edge of the tide, hovering out over the waves to make the most of an offshore wind. I never did see what it was trying to catch. I wondered if mice and especially voles are given to rummaging for food in seaweed. Orkney has its own sub-species of field vole after all, so I suppose that simply by the very nature of Orkney they will turn up near the coast sooner or later. And if it happens there, why shouldn't it happen along the coasts of a narrow projection of land like the Suisnish headland of south Skye? Still, it's not every day I get to see a barn owl adrift over the wavetops.

I settled on the clifftop with my back to a crumbled old stone wall no higher than my head when I sat against it. My view was as raw and compelling as almost anything I have ever seen, and far, far beyond anything I might describe as simply beautiful, for there was a palpable suppressed power on the landscape that only seemed to strengthen as daylight yielded. The sky paled to almost white in the north-west, and everything that was rock in all its forms darkened to a troubling blue-black and seemed to advance en masse, as if it made a conscious animal effort to exaggerate its physical presence to every watching eye and listening ear, like a wolf pack when it howls.

My fondness for the gloaming is a companionable match for watching owls, likewise my capacity for sitting still and doing nothing at all whenever I think I may have contrived circumstances conducive to persuading nature to reveal something of itself. I said I do nothing at all; that's not quite true, I tune in, concede some of my formal human-ness, become landscape. I reasoned the owl would be back. I sat still. I watched the mountains. I waited. It took longer than I thought it might, perhaps an hour, by which time the sky had given up the ghost on daylight and summoned the moon up and out of the ocean.

Ghostly analogies are everywhere in the literature of barn owls, and if that shows a lack of imagination among many generations of scribes it is an understandable lack, for mostly barn owls wear ghostly shades, mostly they are seen in the half-light or in no light at all, mostly they move with what most of us think of as a ghost's gait, and mostly they startle us. Such traits are impressive enough in the hum-drum shadowlands of an old Lowland farmyard. But out here, out where the landscape of the dusk summons to its cause the aura of ocean-reflected, mountain-bestrewn moonlight, and what with my choice of seat within the ruins of a Clearances village happed in its own shroud of threnody, the owl when it finally materialised like a wad of blossom on a wind-crippled runt of a rowan tree not ten yards away dragged a gasp from me, which by the time it had escaped into the open air was most of the way to being a small shout of astonishment.

It was immediately obvious that owl and rowan tree were familiar collaborators, the chosen perch offering clear sightlines along several alleys between old stone walls, alleyways such as a mouse or a vole might use to navigate their ways through the island night. But the barn owl can also turn its head through 180 degrees so that it instantly homes in on the slightest noise behind its back. So for a small eternity the owl surveyed its portion of the island from the rowan, and only its head moved. When it flew at last it travelled no more than the length of the tree's moonshadow before it fell, feet first, and as it fell it disappeared behind the far wall of the ruin where I sat, so that I saw nothing at all of what happened next until, with a wide banner of white wings and a scuffle of talons it announced itself on the topmost stone of the ruin's broken gable. A vole hung from the beautiful heart-shaped face, held there by the odd curve of its broken back.

Whatever I had expected, it was not that. Some startled gesture of mine must have conveyed itself the length of the ruin to the owl, and it was gone almost before I had time to acknowledge that it had arrived. I would imagine that it was as startled as I was. Then just as suddenly the darkness seemed to fall like a dropped shroud. Then the moon climbed above the Cuillin ridge, a heaven-sent moon for a hunting owl and for the owl-watcher with a long walk home.

BARN OWL

⊙ ⊙ ⊙

AND I REMEMBERED THEN that time after time
during the barn owl years at Jerah in the Ochils,
the owl's first evening flight was from the nest in
the chimney to the rowan tree at the front of the
old cottage. This is an old relationship in Scotland,
because the barn owl makes a habit of nesting in
the abandoned nests of mankind, and many of the
ruins are of homes and barns that belong to an era
that insisted on planting a rowan just outside to
ward off evil and to foster good fortune. Now, it is
mostly the owl's good fortune that a rowan stands
just beyond where a door once stood.

Strange: the golden eagle, with no interest in
ruins whatever, indeed a bird that will go to some
lengths to avoid humankind and its works, almost
always chooses a ledge with a nearby rowan for a
nest site, and often weaves the greenery of rowans
into the eyrie itself. No-one knows why, or ever will.
Indeed, it is quite possible that the Gael acquired
the habit from the eagle.

ENCOUNTERS IN THE WILD

The Ochils are rounded, grassy hills the colour of straw in winter and green in the summer. Only the momentary panache of autumn and the midwinter snows relieve their monochrome garb, those and the few trees that thicken the cleughs and sykes* that carve up the hillsides and sometimes separate the hills from each other. But grassy hills are perfect for voles and therefore grassy hills with old stone ruins are perfect for barn owls. Short-eared owls like them too, and being ground nesters, don't care about the ruins. But the lives and the breeding success of both owl tribes are critically dependent on the short-tailed field vole in particular, a species prone to population crashes every few years, with consequent abrupt breeding failure among owls. It is an ancient truth of nature: an abundance of predators is only possible if there is a superabundance of prey. (Thus, there is no such thing as "too many buzzards/sparrow-hawks/ospreys/harriers/eagles", the oft-heard cry of the landowning tribes and their hapless

---

* *Cleugh* – the steep-sided gorge of a burn;
Syke – a wet hollow crossed by a burn.

gun-toting staff.) The short-ear is the most persistently day-flying owl, and only twice in the forty years of my Ochils wanderings have I seen both short-ear and barn owls abroad on the same hillside at the same time, and that was a late afternoon of midwinter with the light fading fast.

The ruin of Jerah stands on a slope of a kind of amphitheatre in the hills whose only outlets are a steep and narrow glen in the south-east and a flattish and broader glen to the west with a small reservoir. The barn owls tended to take the way west on hunting flights, and I was accustomed to seeing them hunt the banks of the reservoir and the heathery moor at the mouth of the glen much more often than the steep-sided innards of the hills. The glen leads to more open slopes with bits of good woodland and long views out over the low-lying Carse of Stirling to the mountains beyond. These open slopes were the barn owls' killing fields. But sometimes, if the wind was out of the north rather than the prevailing south-west, a hunting bird might edge round the bulk of the hills and up onto the higher ground of Sheriffmuir, and it was there that it would be most likely to cross the path of the short-ears.

Once, when the owls had chicks at Jerah, I saw one of the adults labouring homewards across the hillside to the north with prey, taking the high road home by the straightest route, but never did I see the outward flight take any direction but low and westward. It was a good nest to watch, from the drystone dyke about twenty yards from the house, eavesdropping on the bizarre vocabulary of snores, snorts, hisses and occasionally a thin terrier-like yap which the birds practise exclusively around the nest. But they hunt alone and in silence. It was also there that I worked out the mystery of the thing that looked like old Brillo pads, that mystery that had endured since childhood and the day I stepped out of bounds into forbidden territory.

All birds of prey cough up pellets of undigested material, usually just fur and bones. In the nesting season, barn owls cough them up where they plan to nest, and that is what the "nest" is made of, the undigested remnants of voles and mice. It is not so much a nest as a compact mat of insulation. When you think of the colossal nest-building labours of eagle or osprey or mute swan, for example, the barn owl is an object lesson in the first principles of architectural recycling.

But I was never that much of a sitter by nests, and I have grown more dissatisfied with the practice over the years. The notable exception has been a particularly wild mute swan nest site where the tendency of the occupants to break most of the field guide "rules" most of the time in the face of sustained natural adversity has enthralled me for more than thirty years. But then most of a mute swan's life cycle is centred around the nest site and its immediate environs. You can't follow swans into the hills. In general, though, what goes on out in the territory of birds that inhabit wild landscapes is much more compelling and more challenging for the watcher, especially if the end product of the watching is to write it down. So once the barn owl had flown from the chimney at Jerah and paused in the rowan (sometimes for moments, sometimes for minutes, once for half an hour while I sat a few yards away, motionless and trying not to breathe out loud) to test the wind or the nature of the evening or whatever else occupies an owl's mind at such a moment, and once it had flown off on its mission, I would hurry through the gate in the dyke to watch and follow its path out into the world beyond.

Its route was unfailingly the same, at least in my limited experience of it. It would fly downhill and close to the trees that throng the gorge of the hill burn, until it reached the gap in the trees where the track crosses the burn by a crude but hefty bridge. There the owl would also cross the burn and there it would vanish, hidden by the trees. I followed with what haste I could muster and sometimes I would catch sight of it again beyond the bridge, far out over the moor or cruising the bottom of the hillsides, and then I would stalk it for as long as the owl and the light permitted.

I longed to meet it on the bridge, just once, to see it swerve into the narrow gap in the trees head-on and drift low above the bridge and beneath the dark canopy of the trees, an intensely white anomaly moving towards me through such a gathering of shadows, then out into the open and the last rays of sunset striking notes of pale pink or pale yellow on its face and breast and underwings. But it never happened that way, and always it left me far behind, diminishing against the western sky.

Now, all that has changed is the degree of decrepitude in the chimney. All the other reasons of why this corner of the Ochils is good for barn owls are still in place. So every May I walk the track out to the ruin of Jerah to see if they have returned. As yet they have not, and every year there is a little less chimney to work with. But there are still big trees by the burn and from time to time winter storms splinter and deform one or two of these, and as long as there are owls nearby to explore the new possibilities of broken-open tree trunks, there is the possibility of return.

THREE

THE POSSIBILITIES OF broken-open tree trunks were the barn owl's first resort for nest sites, as now (after centuries of dependency on the cast-off buildings of the people, and a few decades of woodland edge nest boxes) they are still an option and in some places the preferred option. Here is a quiet corner of the foothills of the southmost Highlands, with a badger sett at its heart. The sett is flanked by yet another hill burn (badgers insist on the proximity of water) contained between two more crumbling dykes and one dilapidated fence, all of which the badgers cross with ease. Beyond these is a swooping grass field with trees on three sides.

The badger knows the barn owl. They are kindred spirits of the half-light and the dark, and like the barn owl, the badger can also unleash upon the most profound night silence a scream to freeze the blood of every creature of woodland and field, hillside and moor and clifftop, and for that matter of every badger-and-owl-watcher. Badger and barn owl are also both occasional, reluctant daylight travellers, reluctant because in daylight they lose most of the advantages that nature has bestowed on them. They meet all the time as they patrol their territory, and less often inside woodland than outside it, ships that pass in the night fields, mostly without so much as a nod of recognition. This very corner of the Trossachs is the only place where I have ever seen them meet head on, or to be more accurate, I did not see the actual meeting but rather the immediate after-math of the meeting.

I was watching a badger sett on a beautiful evening of late May. The usual cast of bit-part players strolled on and off stage delivering their lines flawlessly – roebuck, robin, woodcock, with noises off from cuckoo and drumming snipe – but by 10pm I had not seen a single badger. It happens. Even at the busiest badger setts there are inexplicable blank nights, inexplicable to the badger-watcher that is. It does not mean that no badgers have emerged, only that you have not seen them emerge. On the night in question I decided to give it one more hour, just in case, although I was in a mood of rare pessimism about my chances.

I was also uncomfortable (uncomfortable, that is, by the standards of badger watching in a truly wild landscape, which is not a pursuit for the faint-hearted or the lap-of-luxury-dweller). The wind was from an unusual airt and that ruled out the best vantage point. Instead I was stuck with a fallen beech trunk. It was okay to sit on except that sitting on it offered no view of the sett. Standing on it I could see some of the sett but it was a precarious stance with only flimsy surviving branches for hand-holds. I was standing by the beech, leaning on its fallen trunk and weighing the options when I saw one of the badger cubs squeeze under the fence and pad along beside the burn. The adventurous independence of the cubs at eight or nine weeks is impressive (April births are not rare this far north). Musteline curiosity and courage and a robust attitude to life and all its obstacles seem to be in place from the outset.

Here was the diversion I was looking for. I decided to follow it. In wellies and waterproof trousers I simply walked down the burn until I reached the point where I had seen the cub squirm under the fence. But it had already negotiated the maze of rocks that once constituted a wall and the burn which was about four feet wide. I felt the volume of water that tugged at my boots where I stood and wondered why the cub had not been tossed a few yards downstream with a skinful of broken bones for its trouble. Instead, there it was at the top of the easier grass slope on the far side of the burn. It stood there for a few seconds, a tiny silhouette. Then it moved off downhill into the brave new world of the field, and I stepped out of the burn and followed.

Possibly until this very moment, the badger cub had never seen such a place. There had been the first dark underground weeks, then the first stumblings in late evening light around the sett, then the first explorations of the closed-in, tree-shadowed, brackeny limits of the clearing. Then the evening came when it dared its first crossing of the burn, the climb up the far bank, then the first sight of the field and a blazing evening sky stopped it in its tiny tracks.

The cub was also about to make another discovery, one that would confer on the field the status of the promised land. One scoop of a clawed foot, one brief foray of a questing snout in the soft earth, and it had tapped into a lifetime's supply of what it is that a badger loves best in all the wild world: earthworms. As far as I could tell at a discreet distance among the trees it ate four in its first fifty yards, but those fifty yards took at least ten minutes. A badger cub eating worms does not make spectacular progress. Not only must the worms be found, but every other square inch must be scented and sifted for food or danger or just to satisfy the urge of curiosity that is the badge of all its tribe.

Then, somewhere high up on that hillside field in the last of the light, something triggered the cub's sense of its solitary vulnerability. I had seen and heard nothing untoward, but suddenly the cub turned and ran. It ran as I had never seen anything run before. It's hair stood on end and it looked as if no part of the creature was in contact with the ground. It had just tasted its first worms, now it tasted first fear. It darted into the trees, half rolled down the bank, splashed chaotically through the water, negotiated the broken wall and the fence and vanished into the sett.

So what was that all about? I looked back the way the badger had come and found a pale stirring there, a barn owl working the thick, uncut grass at the field's edge. Between the first taste of worms and the first taste of fear, it transpired that the cub had also seen its first ghost, eerie, long-winged, twilit, silent, and adrift on the air a couple of notches above badger cub eye-level. It is difficult to imagine a more unnerving set of circumstances in which to encounter your first barn owl. The cub had yet to learn that the barn owl is a mouser to trade, that the owl considers the badger – even at cub dimensions – altogether too fero- cious to tangle with. And it is just possible that the badger – even a fully grown boar – considers the sight of the barn owl (and sight is the least accom- plished of the badger's senses) just too unearthly for its liking and keeps its own distance.

And if the badger knows the barn owl, then so does the badger-watcher. I was sitting on the same fallen tree in another season, and had taken some trouble to adjust my position to snuff out the wind that had been nibbling in an unendearing way at my left ear. I had let my eyes and ears rove around the wood, and I had grown still. I had become a fragment of the woodland dusk myself. That, at least, was how I imagined I appeared to the natives of the wood, until something unsettled me, and whatever instinct had alerted me to whatever it was also commanded me to duck and hunch my shoul- ders. At that moment a large, pale blur appeared from above and behind my head, banked sharp left along the line of the fallen trunk and vanished the way it had come. As it banked and came into focus, it became a barn owl, and the wordless cry that escaped from my lips – "Uhh!" – was the most unworthy sound I have ever uttered either in the company of a barn owl or in the confines of a woodland dusk.

It was then that I realised I had heard nothing at all. When a mute swan flies, the rhythm throbs heraldically across open water; Sibelius at work on the end of his fifth symphony reached for the horn section to convey the sound. When a golden eagle flies you hear the whuff-whuff-whuff-whuff of windmill sails. Raven wings creak like old hinges. But the barn owl had flown within inches of my head, white legs dangling and kinked in at the knees. It banked in front of my face, and left nothing in its wake but silence, a silence that unnerved me.

But consider this. If the barn owl's flight unnerved me, a fairly solidly built six-footer-in-my-boots, imagine the effect it has on voles, mice, rats moles, beetles, moths and frogs. (I have heard it said that they also eat bats and fish, which may be true if the bat is comatose, hanging upside down from a branch or rafter, and the fish has already been killed and dropped by an osprey or an otter; otherwise I don't believe it.) Most of the time, barn owls just eat voles, voles whose only defence is stillness or a risky dash and an ancient inheritance of fear. It is reasonable to assume that, confronted with the kind of flypast I had just been granted, a vole might simply die of fright where it stood.

⊙ ⊙ ⊙

Not far from that badger sett, a minor road crosses a low ridge of hills. In many a dusk I have crossed paths with the local barn owls, and a hunting bird has cut a low swathe through my car's headlight beam or stared from a fencepost as the car crawled past. There is a lay-by near the summit of the road where I am accustomed to pull in, switch off engine and lights, open the window and let the dusky quiet of the place rush in.

The first sound is often a roebuck, typically four harsh gutturals delivered from the same place, then four more, travelling, coming closer. The edge of a plantation forest is just over my right shoulder; he's in there and he may be coming out. The binoculars are already on the passenger seat, their accustomed place whenever I cross that road at barn owl time.

So the roebuck walked into view, head turned away from me and towards the west. He walked in a gentle arc towards the roadside fence, which he cleared from a standing start. He stopped in the middle of the road with his chest facing east, his head south. I was to his north. He turned his head again to face west along his spine, then (a thing I have not seen before in many years of roe deer watching) turned it again to look north across his back – he had turned his head and neck through 270 degrees.

Then the owl.

It came from the same direction as the buck, and as it also crossed the fence between the buck and the car, the buck's gaze followed it until he had to turn his head and neck back the way it had come to face east where the owl perched on a fencepost across the road. So now I know how far a roebuck can turn his head, and the point at which he can go no further.

The owl, unconcerned by deer or car, began to study the grass beyond the fence with its back to me. In the glasses and the very last of the light, I saw it tip forward, open its wings, and drop a yard to a soft thud in the grass.

But it was up out of the grass almost at once with nothing to show for the pounce. Then it flew in tight curves, quartering the open ground of grass and clear-felled tree roots, never more than a yard above the ground, dipping a wing-tip, lifting again, resuming, head-down hunter of the dusk. Then it rose abruptly into the bare branches of a dead birch and perched.

Then it screamed.

If you didn't see that coming, if you didn't know that banshee sound was in its repertoire, if you knew only the owl of the unsettling silence, God knows what you might make of it. I turned briefly to look at the deer, but it had gone.

Another car appeared on the road going too fast and too loud and making smithereens of the dusky calm, the gloaming cut open by main-beam lights with added spotlights. Strange: the owl screams and immediately deepens the power of the silence that follows. The car roars and immediately wrecks what was there before, and the noise lingers and rises and falls as it follows the rises and falls and curves of the road. The smell of its exhaust drifts in the open windows. What now?

I put the glasses on the tree: nothing. I checked all the fenceposts: nothing.

But there was something by the edge of the road that wasn't there before – the owl, facing the grass verge, but lying, not standing. I walked over, bent down slowly, touched it gently: nothing. I turned it over. There was no blood, no mark. No sign of life either. I was just a few miles from the home of a friend who is better at looking after road casualties than I am. I put my hands beneath the warm belly of the owl and carried it back to the car with all the solemnity of an undertaker.

I made a cushion of a fleece jacket on the back

seat and laid it there. As I drove off I was seething with a dangerous cocktail of anger and contempt for the driver of the other car, but I had not gone far when the owl appeared on the headrest of the passenger seat. I put my left arm out, a reflex action, and I felt the talons grip and bite. The pain was extraordinary.

Bringing a moving car to a standstill without the use of my left hand was a new experience in my life. It is far more difficult than it sounds, and far more difficult still when your left wrist has a traumatised owl's talons embedded in it. I opened the passenger window from the controls on the driver's door. I leaned the owl towards the window. Perhaps it would fly from there? It would not. I didn't want to risk bringing it back into the car so that I could exit by the driver's door, so I swung my legs over the gear lever, and (again, one-handed) achieved a gruesome exit through the passenger door.

Out in the night air again, the owl showed no inclination to let go. I tried to prompt it with a few gentle upward gestures of my left hand and arm. The owl held on.

I took it over to the fence, put my hand beside a post, and it simply stepped off. The relief as it relinquished its grip was as indescribable as the pain.

I backed off to the car where I slowly calmed down. I watched the motionless owl on the fence post for ten minutes. What did it make of what had just happened to it? Was it aware of a brush with death, of rescue, of anything at all other than those things that are strictly necessary to survive from day to day, night to night? Was it doing the same as I was – calming down?

Suddenly it flew, following the line of the fence, then a low arc just above the grasses. It flew past the car's open door not ten feet away. It is the silence of the flight that unnerves.

◉ ◉ ◉

THIS IS ALSO osprey country. The wider Trossachs area, and especially embracing the Lake of Menteith, sustains more ospreys than anywhere else in Scotland outwith Strathspey. It was not always thus. When the first two birds turned up here in the early 1970s after an absence of a hundred years or so, I was one of a small group of volunteers who maintained an all-night vigil to try and thwart egg thieves. The nest could hardly have presented a more tempting target, the top of an old dead stump of a tree not twenty feet high. All they would have needed was a ladder. After a couple of years the surrounding plantation trees grew too tall and the ospreys moved to the summit of a huge conifer where they prospered.

Osprey also knows barn owl. This I discovered – emphatically – at four in the morning, sitting on sentry duty outside a "camouflaged" tent (it was dirty green, its only virtue) that had failed to keep out the night's light rainfall but rather had accommodated it in a small pool near my head during the hours when I had been failing to sleep. We worked in pairs and in shifts and it was with some relief that I emerged about 3am into the now dry and awakening world outside. Watchers were commanded to stillness by the circumstances: the tent was pitched in the only possible place with a view of the eyrie tree a hundred yards away, and with no cover whatsoever. There was, for example, a simple rule about going to the toilet – do it in the dark. But that insistence on daylight stillness also brought rewards, as stillness in nature's company always does. At four o'clock the sun was just under the horizon and one of those rewards was a barn owl.

I became aware of it because I was watching the sitting osprey and the osprey had spotted it. Her attitude suddenly changed from relaxed to agitated, taut. Her head was up and craning and she gave voice, not exactly an alarm call but a cry that held (it seemed to me) an edge of challenge, and she was staring at something to my left. I thought perhaps the male was approaching with an early morning fish, but the call was wrong. I turned my head to follow her line of inquiry and there was the owl, coming my way, fifty yards away at head height, closing. That startling moment would inform my appreciation thirty years later of the badger cub's terror – my first head-on view of being stalked by a ghost too.

BARN OWL

The owl sheared off when it was about twenty feet away from me, by which time I had seriously begun to wonder how I might defend myself. But the owl was simply a little slower than I had expected in identifying my seated shape, and it took immediate avoiding action once it recognised me for what I was. It gave me and the tent a hard stare and a wide berth, and in the same silent and unhurried gait it flew in a gentle climbing arc behind me and turned towards the osprey tree where the sitting female watched it every yard of the way. When it passed the tree it was absolutely at the osprey's eye-level. They simply looked at each other in passing, then the owl was gone.

From beginning to end, it was one of the more curious moments I have spent in nature's company, and recollection of the incident now comes complete with a *frisson* of recognition, recognition of the inadequacy of my response to the moment: I was pondering how to defend myself! Now I would burn the buoyant, bouncing beauty of the flight deep into my mind and at the first possible moment, I would try and write it down.

But this I know. The barn owl and the osprey take notice of each other, and there may be no other reason for it than that they are both white-faced, white-breasted, white under-winged conspicuous birds. And in that particular circumstance, the osprey had just set up home in the barn owl's territory, and the owl would never have seen anything like it before. By now, however, there are many ospreys in the barn owl's spring and summer landscape, and the barn owl will know the osprey is a fish eater and the osprey will know the barn owl is a mouser, and each will know their chicks are not threatened by the other, and while a particularly aggressive male osprey might do all it can to discourage the owl from the core of his territory, the local osprey nests are in much taller trees, and the owl is likely to view the osprey's silhouette with nothing more than a passing unease, and from far below.

AFTERWORD

THE BARN OWL (*Tyto alba*) is widespread through much of the world, excluding only the far north and the far south. It is widespread in mainland Britain too, although its population at any one time is mostly guesswork. It is the most recognisable of our owls although the tawny owl is much better known (it's the one that hoots). But the barn owl's striking plumage – pale gold upper wings, back and head, often mottled with silver or bluish-grey details, and white face, breast, under-wings and long dangling legs – make it impossible to mistake for any other species. But a variant, *Tyto guttata*, in mainland Europe has darker plumage and in some cases, no white plumage at all, and these occasionally turn up along our east coast just to keep birdwatchers on their toes.

The barn owl is primarily nocturnal although it is often visible at dawn and dusk, occasionally in daylight too. But it is supremely adapted to hunt at night with extraordinary eyesight, virtually silent flight, and (as with all owls) its ears are asymmetrically positioned on the side of its head creating a short time-lag between two pulses of sound, an arrangement that facilitates pinpoint accuracy in locating prey on the darkest night. Then, it looks supernaturally white in flight, an illusion assisted by its equally supernatural silence. In daylight, hunting when food is scarce or when it must service the demands of a large brood of chicks in the nest, the wings seem disproportionately long (85cm – almost three feet) for the compact size of head and body.

The barn owl is a fusspot with very specific requirements. The nest must be sheltered and ready-made, for it builds nothing at all (that matt of regurgitated pellets hardly amounts to any known definition of "building"). So it likes holes in hollow trees, recesses in caves, the roof spaces of old buildings like barns, church towers, belfries, broken down chimneys, but it also takes readily to well-designed and thoughtfully sited nest boxes.

But it is even fussier with its diet. Its wellbeing in any one year is inextricably linked to the wellbeing of field voles, its principal source of food. Alas for states of wellbeing, vole populations are notorious for chaotic fluctuations. In any period of three or four years there is likely to be a population crash and a population boom known as a "vole plague year". Barn owl conservation is among the most inexact of sciences because the bird's response is frankly perverse. When the voles crash, instead of saying, "okay, no voles this year, let's hammer the pipits", many birds (sometimes the great majority) simply decide not to breed at all, thereby eradicating the problem of feeding young mouths. Then, in vole plague years, the barn owls will start breeding early, lay big clutches (seven or eight eggs is not unusual), often try for two or even three broods, indulge in a little polygamy, and they can be found in the nest in every month of the year. All of which creates population earthquakes that nudge the upper reaches of the Richter scale, hence the guesswork when it comes to numbers.

A vivid illustration of the phenomenon occurred in 2013 (crash) and 2014 (plague). Surveys of traditional nest sites in 2013 suggested that as few as twenty per cent were occupied. In 2014, the figure was almost one hundred per cent. Thus, the only halfway-useful guide to population trends is to take an average figure of three or four years at a time, on which basis there may be around ten thousand pairs in Britain, with particular strongholds in the south-west of both Scotland and England.

◉ ◉ ◉

THERE IS A DARK SIDE to human interaction with barn owls. A quick internet trawl shows how easy it is to buy a barn owl or two. The trade in captive-bred birds is legal, or at least some of it is. A typical ad: "For sale, barn owls, breeding pair, reluctant sale due to illness. £250." A cynic might read that and think, "Sale due to seller's need for £250." Legal or not, it's not what barn owls are for.

Other facets of contemporary human lifestyle, notably road and rail traffic, kill thousands of barn owls every year. An environmental impact study for the HS2 high-speed rail link between London and Birmingham predicts the loss of the entire breeding population of barn owls within 1.5km of the entire length of the route. And ninety per cent of barn owls found dead on farmland contain rat poison. That is a lot of human predation on a bird we profess to love so much.

Yet love it we do. The centuries-old association with humankind and its architecture has accorded the barn owl a unique place in our affections and in our conservation endeavours. The Hawk and Owl Trust, the Barn Owl Trust, the Barn Owl Centre, the Barn Owl Conservation Network, the RSPB, the Scottish Wildlife Trust, and many if not all of the county wildlife trusts in England have practical projects to help barn owls. For example, after the desperately low breeding performance in 2013, the Somerset Wildlife Trust launched a campaign to erect a nest box in every one of the county's 330 parishes.

And surely we have turned to the barn owl more than any other creature (except perhaps swans) to embroider the hodden grey cloth of folklore. It's the bird of wisdom, its unexpected appearance is an omen of good luck – or death (it was Wordsworth's "bird of doom"), it's the guardian of the night world (in Gaelic it is *cailleach-oidhche,* the old woman of the night) and a beacon to guarantee safe passage through the underworld, its call summons bad weather but its call during bad weather heralds the end of bad weather. And a barn owl broth is a cure for whooping cough (don't try this at home: apart from anything else, I'm pretty sure it's illegal).

Poets have reached for the barn owl as long as there has been poetry, none more knowingly than Thomas Gray in his matchless *Elegy Written in a Country Churchyard*:

BARN OWL

Save that from yonder ivy-mantled tower
The moping owl doth to the moon complain
Of such as, wandering near her secret bower,
Molest her ancient solitary reign.

If you are unmoved by the flaky nature of folk-lore whenever it dabbles with the natural world, then there is always this simple and essential truth: the barn owl, unlike all other night-flying owls, is the one that we can *see* in the dark, that its unarguable beauty is layered with mystery, and that all of us have a place in our hearts and minds for mysterious beauty. I have known that to be an an essential truth since I was about eight years old.

JIM CRUMLEY is a nature writer, journalist, poet, and passionate advocate for our wildlife and wild places. He is the author of thirty books, and is a newspaper and magazine columnist and an occasional broadcaster on both BBC radio and television.

He has written companions to this volume on the fox, swan and hare, with further ENCOUNTERS IN THE WILD titles planned. He has also written in depth on topics as diverse as beavers, eagles, wolves, whales, native woods, mountains and species reintroductions.

◉ ◉ ◉

Saraband, Suite 202, 98 Woodlands Road,Glasgow, G3 6HB
www.saraband.net

ISBN: 9781908643742

Printed in the EU on sustainably sourced paper. Cover illustration: © Carry Akroyd. Illustration at left from Thomas Bewick's *A History of British Birds* (1804), and on title page from William Yarrell's 1843 book of the same name.